IMOGEN

The Life and Work of Imogen Cunningham

IMOGEN

The Life and Work of Imogen Cunningham

by **Elizabeth Partridge** | illustrated by **Yuko Shimizu**

VIKING

When Imogen was born in 1883,
her father named her after his favorite character in
a play by William Shakespeare. It was hard to get
ahold of books in those days, but he loved to read
and think and imagine.

Imogen had four older sisters and brothers, and after her came five more. They lived in a little house in the steep, hilly woods outside of Seattle, Washington. Imogen's mother was always busy cooking and scrubbing and sewing and caring for the children. Her father was busy too, hauling wood and coal to make enough money to feed everyone.

But he noticed Imogen liked to look at the pictures in his books. In the evenings, he read poems out loud by the light of the fire. Imogen loved to watch the firelight flicker across his face as he read. The rhythm of his voice and the firelight made daydreamy pictures in her mind.

Imogen liked to get away from the noisy, crowded house and wander outside in the peaceful woods. She noticed how deep and rich the light was at dawn and dusk, how the shadows changed as the sun rose and fell. At night, she saw the bright snap of the stars against the dark sky.

In the quiet of the woods, joy and longing and wonder filled her.
With one of her father's pencils, she drew the trees and grasses and flowers.
She tried to capture all their beauty on paper, but something
was missing.

When Imogen was eight, she was old enough to make the long walk to school through the woods to town. Sometimes she saw bear prints, but Imogen wasn't easily frightened. The woods felt safe and welcoming to her.

Imogen's teacher noticed how much Imogen liked to draw and moved her desk to the side of the room, where Imogen could see everyone. She was quick at her lessons, and when she was done, she was allowed to sketch the other students.

At school and at home, Imogen drew and drew, but something was still missing. Even with so many children, Imogen's father also noticed how much she loved to draw. He had a soft spot for his daughter with her red hair and her serious, stubborn ways.

Maybe she needed paints for the soft greens and blues and browns she saw in the woods. But it seemed so selfish to want something just for her.

Finally, bursting with longing, she whispered to her father she would like a paint set. He looked at her in astonishment and asked: Why hadn't she said anything before? He paid thirty-five cents for a paint set, just for her.

One brush stroke after another, Imogen tried to capture the delicate shades of color she saw everywhere.

Imogen's father found an art class for adults when she was twelve, and the teacher was happy for her to join. Every Saturday morning, she learned new techniques. Every week, she practiced. But even with her new paints, something was missing, and she didn't know what.

When Imogen was in high school, her father suggested she would make a good teacher. He wanted all his children—girls and boys—to be able to support themselves.

Imogen didn't want to be a teacher. She didn't want to be a nurse, like one of her older sisters. She didn't want to be home all day like her mother, cooking and cleaning and scrubbing and sewing. But how could she earn a living?

One day, Imogen saw a magazine article about a woman named Gertrude Käsebier. She was a painter who had studied art in Paris, France, and then discovered photography. She took photographs of people to earn a living and made other photographs for the joy of it. "I am thirsty to do it for my own sake," Käsebier said, "to express what there is in me."

THE LADIES' HOME JOURNAL

Vol. XVIII. No. 6   PHILADELPHIA, MAY 1901

The Foremost Women Photographers of America

A SERIES OF BEAUTIFUL PHOTOGRAPHS
SHOWING WHAT AMERICAN WOMEN
HAVE DONE WITH THE CAMERA
Posed by Frances Benjamin Johnston

MRS. GERTRUDE KÄSEBIER

It struck Imogen like a thunderbolt: This was what she had been missing. Käsebier's photos, with their silvery light and deep shadows, made Imogen sure she wanted to be a photographer. And she noticed something else. She saw that a woman could follow her dreams and earn a living at the same time.

Week after week, Imogen worked as a nanny. She saved every cent she earned until she had fifteen dollars, then sent the money to a company on the other side of the country. They sent her back a camera, a box of negatives made of glass, and a booklet of instructions.

Filled with excitement, Imogen
set up her new camera. *Click* went the
shutter as she captured the image.

When she had exposed all of the negatives, she sent them
back across the country. She waited while they processed the
negatives in chemical baths.

She waited again while they printed the images on photo
paper. It was messy and complicated to use all the chemicals
in the darkroom, so most people didn't mind waiting. Imogen
minded.

Finally, the photographs arrived. There on paper was almost
what she had been dreaming of.

So close.

Imogen knew she needed to unlock the mysteries of the darkroom chemicals. She had to bring out the shades of light and shadow herself.

She had to bring out the shades of light and shadow *within* herself.

She told her father about what she had been missing, and about her dream to make photographs for a living.

"Why do you want to be a photographer?" he asked her. He worried this serious, stubborn daughter of his had an impractical dream. How would she ever support herself taking photographs?

But he loved her, so he made her a darkroom. He emptied the woodshed in the backyard and put in a floor, walls, and a door. He tacked black paper to the walls and ran a pipe with cold water back to the building so she could set up the chemical baths.

Imogen and her friends went out in the woods and read poetry to one another. She draped them in gauzy fabrics and took photographs as they acted out the poems.

Inside her darkroom, she developed the negatives and made prints, then hung them up to dry.

There it was, right in the photographs, all the soft cadence of the poetry, all the beauty, all the feelings she carried deep inside her. Nothing was missing.

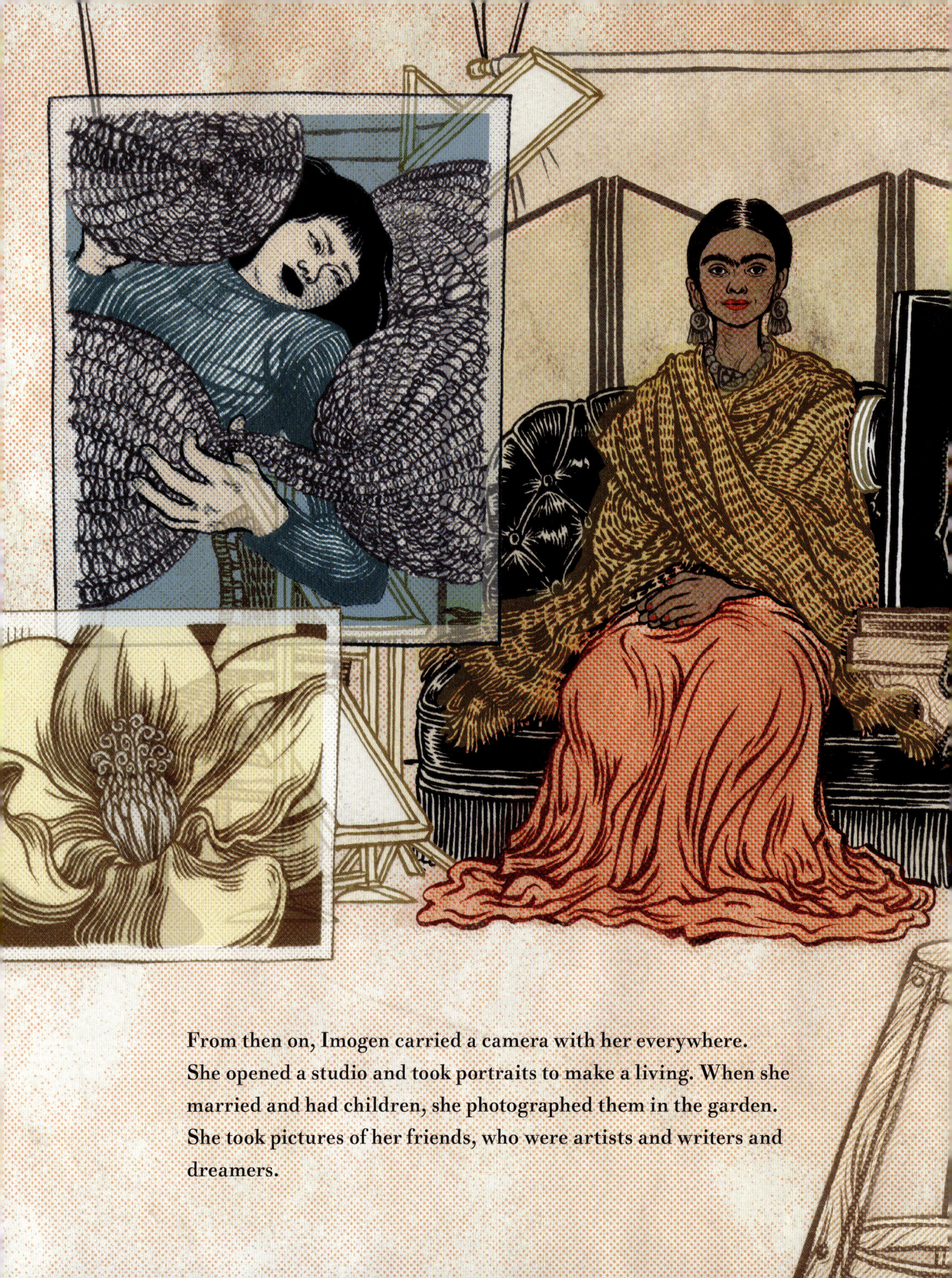

From then on, Imogen carried a camera with her everywhere.
She opened a studio and took portraits to make a living. When she
married and had children, she photographed them in the garden.
She took pictures of her friends, who were artists and writers and
dreamers.

Sometimes poems danced through her mind as she photographed.

"My soul is alight with your infinitude of stars," wrote the poet Tagore. "Your world has broken upon me like a flood.

The flowers of your garden blossom in my body. The joy of life that is everywhere burns like an incense in my heart."

When Imogen's father turned ninety, she took a picture of him sitting on a pile of wood he had just split to stay warm for the winter ahead.

It was a quiet, thoughtful photograph of her father, who liked Shakespeare and thinking and imagining. Maybe it was Imogen's way of saying what was in her heart: *Thank you for believing in me.*

Imogen kept photographing when she was old herself, as old as her father had been. She photographed reflections in windows and mirrors and caught long shadows at the end of the day. She experimented by combining two images into one photograph.

Across America and Europe and Asia, galleries and museums exhibited her photographs, from the earliest to the very latest. People stood and stared and felt all the joy and longing and wonder that Imogen had captured.

Young women saw they could follow their dreams and earn a living as well.

Of the many, many photographs Imogen had taken, people often asked: Which one was her favorite? That was easy for Imogen to answer. "The one I'm going to take tomorrow," she always replied.

Self Portrait with Camera, late 1920s.

AUTHOR'S NOTE

IMOGEN CUNNINGHAM was my grandmother. To me, she was always very old, and always a photographer. Cameras and taking photographs and making beautiful prints were all woven so deeply in her, it was impossible to separate Imogen from her photography. Photography was not something she did; it was who she was.

There were photos everywhere in her tiny San Francisco house: laid out on the dining room table or in piles on chairs. Out the kitchen door and down the rickety back stairs was her darkroom, tucked under the house. The ceiling was too low and the room too small for anyone but Imo.

I learned to watch my grandmother in the garden with her plants, or when we were out together on the steep, busy streets. I wanted to see what she was noticing, see what caught her eye. "I don't hunt for things," she said. "I just wait till something strikes me." Ordinary moments that I overlooked would capture her attention: someone counting out change in the palm of their hand or the zigzagging shadow of outside stairs against a wooden building.

When I was a teenager, I'd take the bus to her house to spot prints for her. Using a delicate brush and silvery-gray inks, I would cover the little flecks of white or black left on the finished print from a bit of dust in the enlarger or a scratch on the negative. Imo would make us a simple lunch—a salad and crusty French bread with butter—and we'd sit on the back porch in the afternoon sun and talk. "How *are* you?" she would always ask me, and she really wanted to know.

She'd tell me about herself as well, and sometimes about her father, Isaac Burns Cunningham. After enlisting in the Union Army in what he called the "War Between the States," he'd returned home to Missouri when the South surrendered. He soon moved to Texas but thought it was "heaven for men and dogs, but hell for women and cattle." He took off again, this time for the Pacific Northwest. There he became a lifelong vegetarian and theosophist, believing in the kinship of all people and that every action, feeling, and thought we have can contribute to the well-being of all others.

Imogen told me how, early in her career, she'd photographed her husband, Roi Partridge, nude on Mount Rainier. The photos immediately created a scandal, and she was branded an "immoral woman" in the press. She didn't let that stop her from following her passion—to photograph anything and everything that caught her eye.

In 1917 she and Roi moved to the San Francisco Bay Area. With three small boys, she concentrated on photographing the plants in her garden and her children, making some of her most luminous photographs. As soon as the boys were older, she took her camera with her as she walked around the city, photographing scenes and people that others overlooked. Her early street photography changed people's perceptions about what was worth photographing: She took pictures of children playing on the street, messy shop windows, and soaring industrial buildings. When her artist friends dropped by, she would often ask them to sit for a portrait. She even pushed the limits of the camera as far as she could: After taking a photograph, she would sometimes wind back the film and take another photograph, creating a double exposure.

To earn a living, Imogen willingly did the hard work of running a portraiture studio, sometimes lugging her heavy portrait camera and tripod on the bus to her clients' homes to photograph them in their own environment. At night she would develop the film, and the next

My Father at Ninety, 1936.

day make prints and deliver them to her clients. When *Vanity Fair* magazine asked her to photograph Hollywood movie stars, she didn't hesitate. Each time an assignment came in, she gathered up her heavy equipment and took the train from Oakland to Hollywood.

One of Imogen's twin sons, Rondal, would become a photographer, as well as my dad. Like Imogen, he adored Isaac and often told me stories about him: how Isaac was teaching himself advanced mathematics in his eighties, and how he eked out a living farming a small apple orchard. Once, when Ron was walking a country road with Isaac, they came across a

The author as a baby with her mother, 1952.

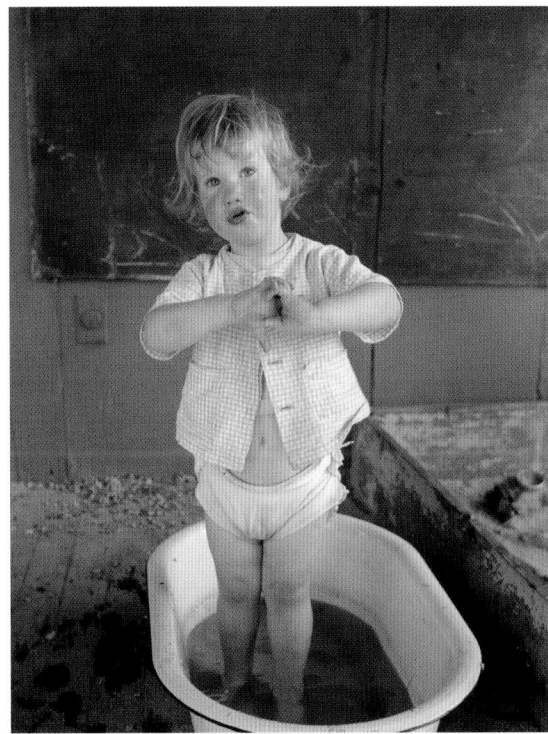

The author's sister, Meg, 1955.

farmer beating his old horse, who was struggling to pull a plow. "Stay your hand!" Isaac yelled, scrambling into the field. He bought the horse on the spot and took it home to live out its days in comfort.

Isaac's deep feelings of kindness and kinship were reflected in Imogen. She joined early civil rights and peace marches and photographed widely, refusing to confine herself to any one group of people. Her friends and assistants were all different ages and from all walks of life. In 1950, when Imogen was sixty-seven, Ron burst into her house saying, "I've just met someone you've got to know!" He introduced her to the Japanese American artist Ruth Asawa. Though Ruth was just out of college, she and

Imogen became lifelong friends, sharing dinners, celebrating birthdays, and arranging sessions so Imogen could photograph Ruth and her latest looped wire sculptures.

Though Imogen was busy with her work, she always took the time to support and mentor young artists, knowing how hard she'd worked to be taken seriously as a photographer. She'd started early; in 1913, she'd written a trailblazing article urging equality for women in the male-dominated photography world—seven years before she, like all American women, even had the right to vote in elections.

When I would visit Imogen in the 1960s and early seventies, young photographers would make pilgrimages to her house, clutching

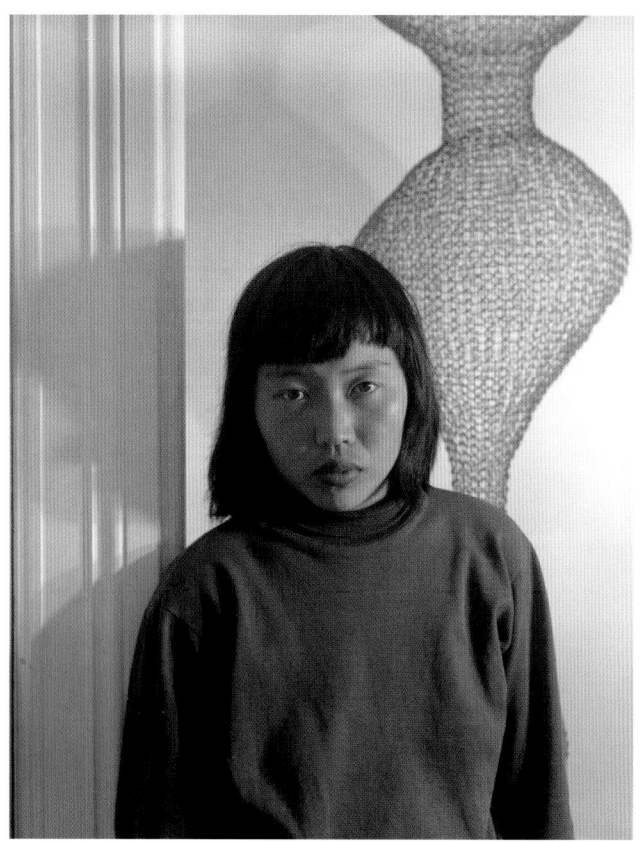

Ruth Asawa and Her Wire Sculpture, 1956.

Frida Kahlo Rivera, Painter, 1931.

their portfolios. She would invite them in, look over their work, and offer them encouragement and advice.

Today, important national and international museums like the Museum of Modern Art (MoMA); the Museum of Fine Arts, Boston; the Getty Museum; and the Centre Pompidou have her photographs in their permanent collections. Artists young and old flock to see her exhibitions, inspired by both her pioneering photographs and her fierce determination to live life by her own rules.

Walking and talking with Imogen, sharing lunch on the back porch, I was learning to love

the world in all its beauty and complexity, and to see the ordinary as transcendent. I understood how important it was that I take all the feelings I had inside and find the best way to express them—in photographs, paintings, words, or music; the medium didn't matter. The path for me led to writing, the joy of finding just the right words to say what is in my heart.

Even now, every few years, Imogen comes to me in my dreams, always with the same question: How *are* you? I never see her, just hear her voice, and I wake up reminded of the beauty she saw everywhere.

Hands with Aloe Plicatilis, 1960.

ENDNOTES

"I am thirsty . . .": Giles Edgerton, "Photography as an Emotional Art: A Study of the Work of Gertrude Käsebier," *The Craftsman* 12, no 1 (April 1907): 90.

"Why do you want to be . . .": Rondal Partridge, in conversation with the author, n.d.

"My soul is alight . . .": Harriet Monroe and Alice Corbin Henderson, eds., *The New Poetry: An Anthology* (New York: The Macmillan Company, 1917), 330.

"The one I'm going . . .": James Danziger and Barnaby Conrad III. *Interviews with Master Photographers: Minor White, Imogen Cunningham, Cornell Capa, Elliott Erwitt, Yousuf Karsh, Arnold Newman, Lord Snowdon, Brett Weston* (New York: Paddington Press, 1977), 54.

"I don't hunt for things . . .": Imogen Cunningham, interview by her son Rondal Partridge, recorded on quarter-inch audio tape, San Francisco, California, 1972.

"heaven for men and dogs . . .": Edna Tartaul Daniel, "Imogen Cunningham: Portraits, Ideas, and Design" (transcript of 1959 interview), Berkeley, California: Regional Oral History Office, University of California, Berkeley, 1961, 3.

"Stay your hand!": Rondal Partridge, conversation.

"I've just met someone . . .": Rondal Partridge, conversation.

TIMELINE OF LIFE AND WORKS

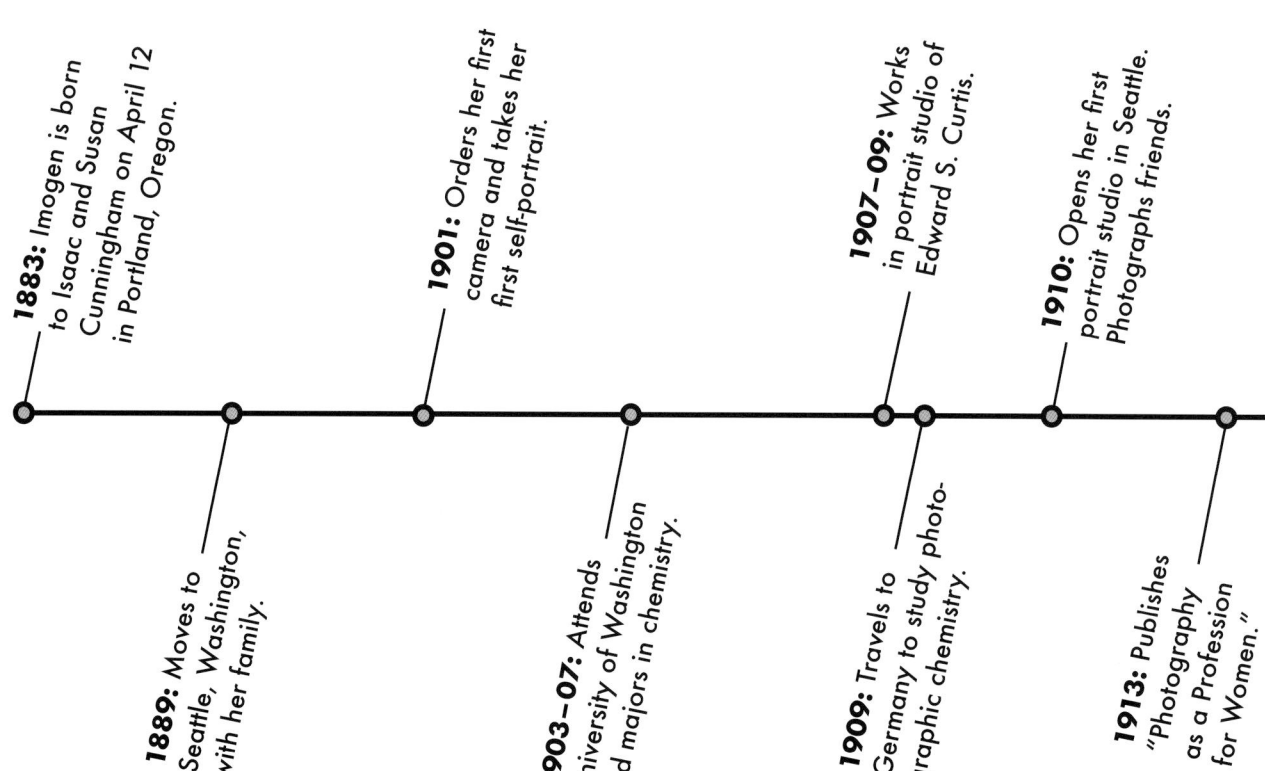

1883: Imogen is born to Isaac and Susan Cunningham on April 12 in Portland, Oregon.

1901: Orders her first camera and takes her first self-portrait.

1907–09: Works in portrait studio of Edward S. Curtis.

1910: Opens her first portrait studio in Seattle. Photographs friends.

1889: Moves to Seattle, Washington, with her family.

1903–07: Attends University of Washington and majors in chemistry.

1909: Travels to Germany to study photographic chemistry.

1913: Publishes "Photography as a Profession for Women."

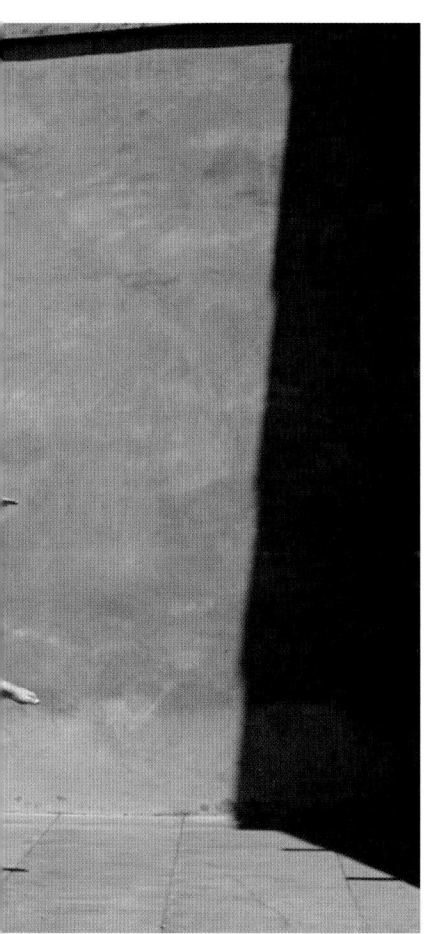

LEFT: *Boy in New York, 1956.* CENTER: *Three Dancers, Mills College, 1929.* RIGHT: *Double Dutch, New York City, 1956.*

1915: Marries etcher Roi Partridge. Son Gryffyd is born.

1917: Moves to San Francisco. Twins Rondal and Padraic are born.

1920s: Photographs primarily plants and her family.

1923: Makes her first double exposure.

1931: Becomes founding member of photography association Group f/64.

1934: Marriage ends in divorce. Begins documentary street photography.

1935–76: Supports herself as a portrait photographer. Continues her fine art practice and exhibits at major art museums worldwide.

1970: Is awarded a Guggenheim Fellowship.

1976: Takes photographs for a photography book. Dies June 23 in San Francisco.

For my granddaughter, Lila Imogen Ratcliff-Pham   —E. P.

To all the children who have passion to create and to all the parents
who want to nurture their children's curiosity and creativity   —Y. S.

VIKING
An imprint of Penguin Random House LLC
1745 Broadway, New York, New York 10019

First published in the United States of America by Viking,
an imprint of Penguin Random House LLC, 2025

Text copyright © 2025 by Elizabeth Partridge
Illustrations copyright © 2025 by Yuko Shimizu

All photographs © 2025 Imogen Cunningham Trust /
Courtesy ImogenCunningham.com
Photographs on page 35 courtesy of the author
Ruth Asawa and Her Wire Sculpture, 1956
Artwork © 2025 Ruth Asawa Lanier, Inc. / Artists Rights Society (ARS), New York, courtesy of David Zwirner

Visit us online at PenguinRandomHouse.com.

Library of Congress Cataloging-in-Publication Data is available.

ISBN 9781984835185

1   3   5   7   9   10   8   6   4   2

Manufactured in China

TOPL

Edited by Tamar Brazis   Design by Jim Hoover
Text set in Acanthus Text OT, Aguila, and Futura Medium

The art for this book was first created with black ink on watercolor paper,
then scanned in and colored using Adobe Photoshop.